the facts about

CAFFEINE

DRUGS **the facts about**
CAFFEINE

LORRIE KLOSTERMAN

𝓂𝒸 **Marshall Cavendish**
Benchmark
New York

This book is dedicated to Paul, who introduced me to café-sitting, cappuccinos, and creative conversation, to which I've been addicted ever since.

Thanks to John Roll, Ph.D., director of Behavioral Pharmacology at UCLA Integrated Substance Abuse Programs, for his expert review of this manuscript.

Marshall Cavendish Benchmark
99 White Plains Road
Tarrytown, NY 10591
www.marshallcavendish.us

Library of Congress Cataloging-in-Publication Data

Klosterman, Lorrie.
The facts about caffeine / by Lorrie Klosterman.
p. cm. — (Drugs)
Includes bibliographical references and index.
ISBN-13: 978-0-7614-2242-6
ISBN-10: 0-7614-2242-0
1. Caffeine—Juvenile literature. I. Title. II. Series: Drugs
(Benchmark Books (Firm))

QP801.C24K56 2006
613.8'4—dc22
2005037351

Photo Research by Joan Meisel

Cover photo: James Marshall/Corbis

The photographs in this book are used by the courtesy of:
Corbis: 1, 2–3, 5; James Marshall: 6, Jose Luis Pelaez, Inc.: 18, 21;
Bettmann: 34; Christine Osborne: 43; Bo Zaunders: 44; Owen Franken: 58;
Howard Sochurek: 62: Joe Bator: 78; Nancy Ney: 82; Images.com: 85;
Ariel Skelley; Peter Arnold, Inc.: 77; Alfred Pasieka: 91; Rosalind
Creasy, Photo Researchers, Inc.: 11; Charles D. Winters: 49; Roger
Harris: 50; Sinclair Stammers: 72; John Bavosi, North Wind Picture
Archives: 15, 28.

Printed in China
1 3 5 6 4 2

CONTENTS

THAT FIRST CUP OF COFFEE TO JUMP START ONE'S DAY IS A RITUAL IN MANY AMERICAN HOUSEHOLDS.

INTRODUCTION

In many households, mom or dad starts off the day with a cup of coffee, perhaps even from a machine that automatically prepares that hot, black brew just as the morning alarm clock goes off. Some people prefer tea, maybe with the delightful aroma of added spices, flowers, or flavorings. For kids, caffeinated soft drinks are an energy-boosting equivalent and a mainstay of virtually every social activity. Of course, many adults drink caffeine-containing sodas, too.

Caffeinated beverages are extremely popular around the globe. It is estimated that people consume a staggering 120,000 tons of caffeine each year, mostly in the form of coffee, tea, and cola beverages (or noncolas to which caffeine has been added). That works out to over one *trillion* cups a year!

Caffeine is such a familiar part of society that it may seem odd to refer to it as a drug, yet a drug it surely is. It is not a naturally occurring substance in the human body, and has an undeniable effect on it. No wonder there have been questions for centuries about whether consuming caffeine is a good idea. Are the temporary effects of caffeine, such as speeding up heart rate, of any concern? Does it cause serious health problems over time? Those concerns continue, especially now that daily caffeine consumption often starts in childhood—even toddlerhood in some families—due to the popularity of soft drinks and sweetened (and often iced) coffee beverages that kids enjoy.

Hundreds of scientific studies have been conducted to answer questions like those, and studies are still searching for clear answers. So far, few serious health problems have been convincingly linked to caffeine when it is used in moderate amounts—a few sodas or cups of coffee or tea a day. Consuming larger quantities for years, or for a lifetime, could be a different story. And ingesting a lot of caffeine can happen unknowingly. For example, a plant called guarana is being added to beverages, energy bars, smoothies, and other products, in the form of "guarana extract." Most consumers don't realize that guarana has a lot of caffeine in it. Most people do know that colas or other dark-colored beverages are likely to have caffeine, but they may not realize that it is added to many noncola beverages, which may be uncolored or brightly colored, such as citrus-flavored sodas. Caffeine also is added to some beverages whose names, such as "vitamin water," offer no suggestion that they contain a stimulant drug.

The story of caffeine is a fascinating tale that reaches back to ancient civilizations, spans the globe, and is wrapped up in politics, religion, social customs, environmental protection, and more. Today, caffeine crops are a major income source for some of the world's poorest countries, and caffeine fuels the fast-paced lifestyles of people in the richest countries. Caffeine's story will continue to evolve as new caffeine-containing concoctions emerge to satisfy a huge demand for this most popular of stimulant drugs.

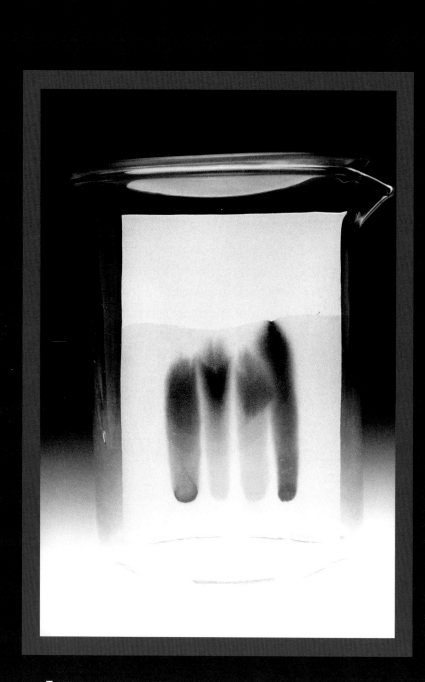

THE CHANCE MEETING BETWEEN A POET AND A SCIENTIST—AND THE SCIENTIST'S USE OF CHROMATOGRAPHY—LED TO THE DISCOVERY OF CAFFEINE.

1 The History of Caffeine

For centuries people have sampled nature's bounty of plants for those that have useful or pleasurable effects. Among them are plants that, when eaten, chewed, smoked, or made into a beverage, increase a person's alertness and energy level. Substances that do so are called stimulants. The most common stimulant drug in use for centuries has been caffeine, yet it wasn't until the 1800s that scientists purified it and gave it a name.

It was a chance meeting between a poet and a scientist that led to the identification of caffeine, in 1819, as the stimulant in coffee. The poet was the world-renowned German writer, Johann Wolfgang von Goethe. Goethe was an intelligent and curious man who had several interests, including a fascination with the sciences. That interest sparked a friendship with a prominent German chemist, Johann Wolfgang Döbereiner. During one of Goethe's visits to Döbereiner's laboratory, he met a young man there, Friedlieb Ferdinand Runge. Runge was a clever young researcher who had recently identified the chemical that makes many plants in the nightshade family poisonous.

Goethe had some whole coffee beans. He handed them over to Runge to see if the chemist could discover a substance responsible for their stimulating effect. Runge had been working out a way to separate chemicals from each other by paper chromatography—something many students today do in chemistry class. Chromatography takes advantage of the ability of liquids to soak into thick paper, even against gravity, if the paper is held vertically. Runge found that when he put paper into a liquid made from a ground-up plant (extract), the many substances in the extract would travel up the paper with the liquid. But some would travel higher than others, which separated them from each other. The paper would then be cut up, and each substance collected and dried. With the aid of that technique, in a few months' time Runge purified a crystalline white powder with a bitter taste, and named it caffeine.

The story of caffeine includes much more than how the chemical was identified. It rightly should include the history of coffee, tea, soft drinks, and other beverages, as well as foods that contain caffeine, but that would take thousands of pages. A few highlights will be presented that may spark a curiosity to learn more from other in-depth sources.

Coffee

There are some holes in the history of how coffee made its way into virtually every culture in the world. Not every historian agrees on exactly what happened or when, but most believe that a man named Dhabhani (a shortened version of his much longer name), played an important role. Dhabhani was a *sufi*, a member of a devout spiritual group within the religion of Islam. Sometime in the mid-1400s, he traveled from his town in the southern end of the Arabian peninsula, known today as the Republic of Yemen, to a part of Africa now called Ethiopia. During his stay, Dhabhani came to enjoy greatly a popular beverage being consumed there—*qahwa*. It was flavorful and it gave him a sense of renewed energy. He brought some back to his home in Yemen and shared it with other sufis. They appreciated how it helped them continue their long hours of prayer.

Eventually, people outside the sufi group tried the beverage, which we now call coffee. They would gather to drink it and to socialize. By the early 1500s, coffeehouses had sprung up in all the large cities of the Arab world. In the centuries that followed, coffee drinking by Islamic people was banned a few times. Sometimes religious leaders argued that Islam's holy text, the Koran, forbade it, as it did alcohol. (Coffee was not specifically mentioned in the Koran, but some people felt that its wording meant that all substances that changed a person's state of awareness were forbidden.) Other times, rulers in power were uncomfortable with the huge popularity of the coffeehouses, where citizens would discuss many different things, including their dissatisfaction with the rulers. Also, having a public place to converse, dine, and be entertained was quite a change in Arab society at the time. Before that, people had mostly stayed at home with their families. Some people were concerned that the coffeehouses were changing social values for the worse.

In spite of the social upheaval coffeehouses caused, people kept coming for the beverage and the banter, and the habit spread to Europe and beyond. In the mid-1600s, England became a major importer of coffee, and coffeehouses flourished there. Students at Oxford University managed to get a local coffeehouse established where they congregated with leading scientists to share ideas, research, and vibrant discussions. That group was the humble beginning of the now world-famous scientific organization, the Royal Society.

England's passion for coffee led to the establishment of British-controlled plantations in those of its colonies that had a suitable climate. Disease among the plants was a recurrent problem, however, so England focused on growing tea, which was less plagued with disease. For that reason tea became a mainstay of British beverages, which it remains today.

The desire for coffee in Europe and elsewhere continued, however, and coffee plantations spread into many of the tropical and subtropical regions of the globe to fill the demand. Today, coffee is grown in dozens of countries, and several varieties are known for their distinct flavors. Countries that grow and export the most coffee today are Brazil, Colombia, Vietnam, Indonesia, India, Mexico, Guatemala, Uganda, Ethiopia, and Peru.

THE PRODUCTION OF COFFEE HAS SPREAD FROM AFRICA THROUGHOUT THE WORLD. HERE, WORKERS HARVEST COFFEE ON A COSTA RICAN PLANTATION.

15

Tea

An impressive manuscript from the Tang Dynasty of seventh-century China, known as the *Ch'a Ching* (*Classic of Tea*) and written by Lu Yu, describes an already well-established devotion to tea drinking. Lu Yu's book explains in great detail the proper ways to grow and prepare tea. But even before that, in the first century BCE, China was cultivating tea rather than just harvesting it from wild plants. In fact, the use of tea as a medicinal beverage is believed to have been discovered three thousand years before that, by the second emperor of China, Shen Nung, possibly from plants near present-day India.

Tea drinking in Japan was introduced at the end of the twelfth century by the Buddhist monk Eisai Myoan while traveling to Japan. It became popular there, not just as a beverage, but as an art form and an expression of the spiritual principles of Buddhism. The preparation, serving, and sharing of tea evolved into a revered ceremony that is still practiced today. Tea drinking gradually spread throughout Southeast Asia. In other countries, such as Korea, special rituals around the preparation and sharing of the beverage have also evolved.

Tea drinking was first brought to Europe in the 1500s, probably by Portuguese travelers to China. It was made popular in England in the 1660s by the Portuguese princess Catherine of Braganza, who became Queen Catherine after her marriage to King Charles II of England. (The "Queens" borough of New York City is named after her.) Over the next few hundred years, tea demand in Europe grew dramatically, until importing enough from China was far too expensive and difficult. So in the 1830s, the British set up tea plantations in India, a British colony at the time. Eventually India came to provide much of the demand of the British Isles and elsewhere (it provided mostly "black" tea, rather than the "green" tea of China).

Tea first arrived in North America in the mid-1700s with Peter Stuyvesant, the Dutch explorer, who brought some to the Dutch settlement of New Amsterdam (later renamed New York). Settlers linked to England, however, like those in Boston, seem to have learned about it a few decades later. Tea came to be widely enjoyed in the colonies until the Boston Tea Party, in 1773. After that, it was considered unpatriotic to drink tea from Britain, and it was then that the histories of tea and coffee intersected because the downfall of tea became the opening for coffee to flourish and eventually become the favorite caffeinated beverage in the United States.

There are many more chapters in the history of tea as it was embraced in Eastern Europe, Russia, and the Middle East. As its popularity grew, so did the number of plantations and the diversity of countries in which it was cultivated. Today, plantations exist outside the plant's original range, in tropical countries within Southeast Asia, Africa, and South America.

Coffeehouses and the American Revolution

Ever since coffee first appeared as a widely enjoyed beverage, the coffeehouses that sprang up to provide it (as well as tea) have been important gathering places where people discuss current affairs. In the Muslim world of the 1600s, where coffeehouses are thought to have first

THE DESTRUCTION OF TEA IN BOSTON'S HARBOR IN THE COLONIAL ERA LED TO THE ASCENSION OF COFFEE AS THE NEW NATION'S CAFFEINATED BEVERAGE OF CHOICE.

become widespread, coffee was even banned because people were coming together to enjoy the beverage, and naturally tended to talk among themselves. Among the topics—like today—were the problems of their society, and what they might do about it. That made the leaders of the time nervous, fearing that citizens might decide to oust unpopular leaders and replace them with their own choices. A century later and far across the Atlantic in colonial America, talk of breaking away from Britain *was* stirring. Not only did the American coffeehouses serve beverages, many had meeting rooms where some of the leading figures in American history gathered to plan a revolution against the crown. Paul Revere and others are thought to have planned the Boston Tea Party of 1773 at the Green Dragon, which was a coffeehouse, tavern (serving alcoholic beverages), and inn in Boston. After that event, in which tons of British tea were tossed into Boston Harbor in rebellion against taxes the Americans were required to pay, coffee became the favored caffeine-containing beverage, and has been so ever since. The Green Dragon is said also to have been a frequent meeting place of the Sons of Liberty, the Boston Committee of Correspondence, and the North End Caucus (whose members included Samuel and John Adams). Each of these groups was important in the revolution. In addition, the coffeehouse hosted a meeting in 1788 during which a petition was created that called for adopting a federal Constitution—the document that would become the foundation of the United States Constitution.

Coca-Cola, the most popular of all soft drinks worldwide, went public in 1886, based on the recipe of pharmacist John Pemberton. Pemberton had a drugstore and soda fountain in Atlanta where one of his potions became popular as a remedy for a hangover from drinking too much alcohol. It was a combination of caffeine (from cola nuts), cocaine (from coca plants), and alcohol, mixed into a thick, sugary syrup and combined with carbonated water to make it fizzy. That was the very first Coca-Cola. Soon the beverage became a favorite, not just of people with hangovers, but among the general population. Word of it spread across the state, and when it became available in bottled form, it won customers all across the country—and eventually, throughout the world.

When Coca-Cola was first created, there weren't any prescription medicines or regulations about what went into potions. Some of them contained dangerous drugs such as opium, morphine, heroin, or cocaine. But in 1906 Congress passed the Pure Food and Drugs Act stating that the ingredients of products had to be listed. Though it didn't yet prohibit any, the act listed substances that were con-sidered habit-forming or "deleterious" (harmful). Coca-Cola's recipe was then changed, removing the cocaine and most of the alcohol. Asa Candler, head of the Coca-Cola Company, considered the caffeine too important a component to alter. Besides, caf-feine was not on the list of harmful ingredients.

COCA-COLA HAS BEEN THE NATION'S FAVORITE SOURCE OF COLD, LIQUID CAFFEINE SINCE IT WENT PUBLIC IN 1886. THIS IS AN ADVERTISEMENT FROM 1903.

Coca-Cola did not become the popular beverage it is today without a fight by the federal government to remove the caffeine, however. A years-long court battle was waged early in the 1900s by Dr. Harvey Wiley, representing the government's Bureau of Chemistry (an early version of the Food and Drug Administration). A key objection was that children, who were avid consumers of the beverage, should not be exposed to caffeine. Obviously, the Coca-Cola Company won that battle, although it agreed to reduce the caffeine content by half, and not to show any child under the age of twelve in advertisements—a promise it kept until 1986.

As other carbonated beverages were invented, caffeine was added to many of them, too, including many of the "uncolas." Now, some soft drinks are available in decaffeinated forms, but those are less popular than the original caffeinated varieties.

Chocolate

Chocolate is enjoyed as a food and beverage by many cultures. The word *chocolate* is used to refer to many different kinds of edible items, but the common ingredient in them all is *cacao* (ka-cow). Cacao refers to the seeds (sometimes called "beans") of a tropical plant whose scientific name is *Theobroma cacao*.

The preparation of cacao to create a beverage originated in the New World tropics before 1000 BCE, and perhaps much earlier. Both the ancient Mayan culture and, later, the Aztecs (in present-day Mexico) thought of cacao as a sacred substance. They even prized the seeds enough to use them as currency. The beverage they made from cacao, called *xocoatl*, consisted of roasted, ground-up cacao mixed with very hot water. To this they added spices, cornmeal, and even hot peppers. The result was a bitter but invigorating drink.

The Spanish conquistador Hernán Cortés learned of cacao from the Aztec emperor Montezuma II and is credited with introducing it to Europe. Christopher Columbus is said to have come across it first and to have brought some seeds back to Spain, though neither he nor the royal family were very interested in them. But in 1528 Cortés brought back not just the seeds but all the materials to make the Aztecs' spicy beverage, and he shared the brew with the Spanish king. It seems that Cortés was the first person to add sugar as well, creating a sweet, delicious concoction that the nobility cherished—and kept secret from the rest of the world, some say, for nearly a hundred years.

The Europeans named the delightful drink "chocolate" (based on the Aztec *xocoatl*). Eventually it became available, and much beloved, throughout the world and among average citizens. Today, chocolate has come to mean a wide array of beverages and foods that have cacao in them, usually in combination with sweeteners, flavorings, or other ingredients.

The Dutch made an important contribution to chocolate's history in 1828 by coming up with a process that removed cocoa butter (the fats) from the cacao, allowing it to mix more easily with water. It is believed that the Englishman Joseph Fry made the first chocolate bar in the mid-1800s. In 1875, a Swiss man, Daniel Peter, created milk chocolate with the aid of inventor Henri Nestlé, and to this day Switzerland makes some of the world's most prized chocolate.

These were just some of the steps in a rich history that led the way for cacao to become the versatile, treasured substance it is today, in its many forms—including being mixed with coffee as a delightful beverage or confection. Meeting the world's cravings for cacao has inspired the spread of plantations beyond the New World tropics, and today the major cacao producers are Brazil, Ecuador, Cameroon, Ivory Coast, Ghana, Nigeria, and Indonesia.

More Caffeine from the Tropics
Other plants besides coffee, tea, cola, and cacao are important sources of caffeine for a worldwide market. Guarana, or guaraná, and maté are two that have been used by indigenous people for hundreds or possibly thousands of years. European explorers who traveled along the Amazon River in the 1800s brought back word of these plants, and the beverages made from them. There is little historical record of guarana use outside of the Amazon region

through the 1800s and 1900s, however, and only in the last few decades has it started showing up as a popular ingredient in "energy" drinks and foods in the United States, Europe, and other industrialized countries. In fact, guarana growers have been having trouble keeping up with the demands from around the world. Maté, too, has been popular as a tea in South America (the Andes region) for centuries, but only in the last few years has it been exported elsewhere in the world in any significant amounts. It is being sold as a "healthier" stimulant drink than coffee because of its many nutrients.

Each of the caffeine-containing plants just described grows in the tropics. As they became commodities of value to the rest of the world, large areas of tropical forest were converted to planta-tions, and indigenous tribes who have lived there were edged out. The plantation workers were often slaves who lived in horrible conditions. A French traveler to the Caribbean islands wrote, in the late 1700s, "I do not know if coffee and sugar are essential to the happiness of Europe, but I know well that these two products have accounted for the unhappiness of two great regions of the world: America [the Caribbean] has been depopulated so as to have land on which to grow them; Africa has been depopulated so as to have the people to cultivate them."

The demand for caffeine today continues to make it profitable for tropical countries to expand plantation lands. Caffeine crops are still harvested

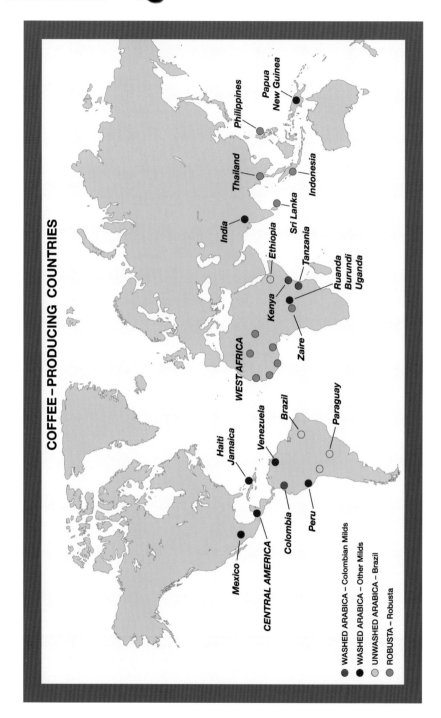

COFFEE–PRODUCING COUNTRIES

Papua New Guinea
Philippines
Thailand
Indonesia
India
Sri Lanka
Ethiopia
Tanzania
Ruanda
Burundi
Uganda
Kenya
WEST AFRICA
Zaire
Haiti
Jamaica
Venezuela
Brazil
Paraguay
Mexico
CENTRAL AMERICA
Colombia
Peru

WASHED ARABICA – Colombian Milds
WASHED ARABICA – Other Milds
UNWASHED ARABICA – Brazil
ROBUSTA – Robusta

by some of the poorest people, while the plantations are owned by the wealthiest. Fortunately, organizations now exist to help get more of the enormous amounts of money spent by caffeine consumers to the plantation workers who provide it. "Fair trade" coffee is now sold at many cafés and stores. That refers to coffee from small family-run farms where the workers are paid a decent minimum wage and work in better conditions than on most large plantations. These farmers also grow their crops in ways that help to preserve the native forests and the wildlife that depend on them.

COFFEE PLANTS ARE QUITE PRETTY TO LOOK AT, AND GIVE NO INDICATION OF THE POWER OF THEIR PRODUCT.

2 WHERE WE GET OUR CAFFEINE

At virtually every social and cultural event, people are offered caffeinated beverages in one form or other. A large survey in the late 1990s revealed that 87 percent of adults and 76 percent of children ages 6 to 17 in the United States consumed caffeine daily. Among adults, coffee was the most popular, making up about 70 percent of the total. Soft drinks made up about 16 percent, and tea, 12 percent. Among children, not surprisingly, soft drinks rather than coffee were the most important source of caffeine. Today, soft drinks may surpass coffee as the most common source of caffeine for all.

Besides coffee, soft drinks, and tea, other sources of caffeine include certain energy drinks and energy bars, coffee-flavored foods, alertness pills, pain medicines, weight-loss products, and a few others. Certain caffeinated products, including maté, guarana, and green tea are marketed as healthier alternatives to coffee because of other substances they contain, such as vitamins, minerals, and antioxidants (chemicals believed by some to lower a person's risk of some illnesses, perhaps including cancer). Chocolate has only a tiny amount of caffeine, though it does contain a related stimulant, theobromine.

This chapter offers a brief explanation of how caffeine-containing plants are processed, and describes the kinds of products that contain caffeine.

Coffee

The plants from which coffee is made belong to the genus *Coffea* (a *genus* is a group of closely related plants or animals). Several types of coffee plants exist in the wild, and all of them like warm temperatures. That explains why the coffee-growing regions of the world are located along Earth's equatorial belt. Some varieties of coffee can tolerate cooler areas better than others, as long as it doesn't freeze and there are no dramatic seasonal changes in temperature. Most types require some shade to thrive, especially as young plants, but some have been bred to withstand a lot of sunlight so they will survive on large plantations where forest trees have been cut down.

Coffee plants can grow to a height of thirty feet, though they usually are trimmed shorter for easier

Caffeine Content of Plants

PLANT	APPROXIMATE CAFFEINE CONTENT (as Percentage of Plant Weight)	PART OF PLANT USED	HOW PREPARED
Coffee	1–2	Seed ("bean"); leaf (sometimes used like tea)	Roasted and brewed as a beverage; added to foods
Tea	3.5*	Leaf, bud dried	Sometimes fermented, brewed as a beverage; added to foods
Cola	1.5	Seed ("nut")	Beverage; chewed whole
Cacao	.03	Seed	Ground for beverages, confections, foods
Guarana	4	Seed	Brewed as a beverage; added to soft drinks and foods
Maté	<1	Seed	Brewed as a beverage

*Though tea leaves have more caffeine than coffee beans *by weight*, only a small weight of tea leaves is used per cup, so the final caffeine content of tea usually is less than coffee.
(Source: Weinberg and Bealer, 2001, p. 236)

harvesting. They have large, dark green leaves and produce delightfully scented, delicate white flowers all year long. Once pollinated, a flower withers, its petals fall, and a green "cherry" develops in its place. A coffee cherry becomes bright red as it ripens, which takes about a year. Then it is picked, dried, and the outer layers (the fruit) are removed to expose a pair of pale green seeds, or "beans." When roasted, the beans become dark brown, oily on the surface, and delightfully aromatic. They are then ground into a powder and combined with hot water to make coffee.

Just two types of coffee are cultivated in large amounts for the world market, *Coffea arabica* and *Coffea canephora*. *Coffea arabica*, which means "coffee shrub of Arabia," provides about 75 percent of today's coffee. It tastes the best, so brings the highest prices to growers. Arabica trees do best at high altitudes where it is not so humid. That adds to the expense of arabica coffee, since it is more work to transport the beans out of the mountains.

Coffea canephora, also known as "robusta," is more resistant to disease, parasites, and humidity. It grows best at lower altitudes, in regions that get about sixty inches of rainfall a year or more and don't have frost. The caffeine content of robusta beans is about twice that of arabica beans, but the flavor is not as good, so they are usually blended with better-tasting arabica or used for instant mixes that have other flavorings.

The amount of caffeine in a cup of coffee depends on many things. These include the type of beans used, how finely they are ground, how much is used per cup, and how the water is passed through the grounds. The average amount of caffeine in a cup of coffee varies widely (as does the amount of liquid defined as "a cup"). An average cup is often said to have 100 mg, but the amount can range anywhere from about 60 to 120 mg.

Soft Drinks and Energy Drinks
The most popular beverages among young people in the United States are carbonated beverages, also known as sodas or soft drinks (as opposed to "hard" drinks, meaning those that contain alcohol). Adults like them too—so much that people in the United States spend around $60 billion a year on soft drinks, which is about 15 billion gallons. That is equivalent to almost two 12-ounce sodas per day for every man, woman, and child in the country. Most sodas contain caffeine.

Coca-Cola was at one time made from syrup that contained extract from cola nuts (a natural caffeine source). Soft drinks today—both "colas" and many noncolas—have caffeine added to them as part of the recipe. That caffeine comes from the vast amounts generated when decaffeinated coffee and tea are made. The decaffeination process is complex, but the principle behind it is to draw out the caffeine by soaking the coffee beans or tea leaves in water, chemical solvents, or other materials.

SOFT DRINKS ACCOUNT FOR ABOUT $60 BILLION WORTH OF SALES IN THE UNITED STATES EACH YEAR.

The amount of caffeine in soft drinks varies, and it usually isn't listed on the beverage container. In general, most have 30 mg to 50 mg per 12-ounce serving—half that of an 8-ounce cup of coffee.

A new sort of caffeinated beverage, called an "energy drink," started appearing on grocery store shelves late in the 1980s. The first was Jolt Cola, with about 70 mg of caffeine in a 12-ounce serving (compared to 30 mg to 50 mg in a typical caffeinated soda). Next came Red Bull (from Austria), based on a beverage from Thailand. One 8-ounce can contains 80 mg of caffeine, plus about five teaspoons of sugar. It was first sold in 1987 and quickly became

34

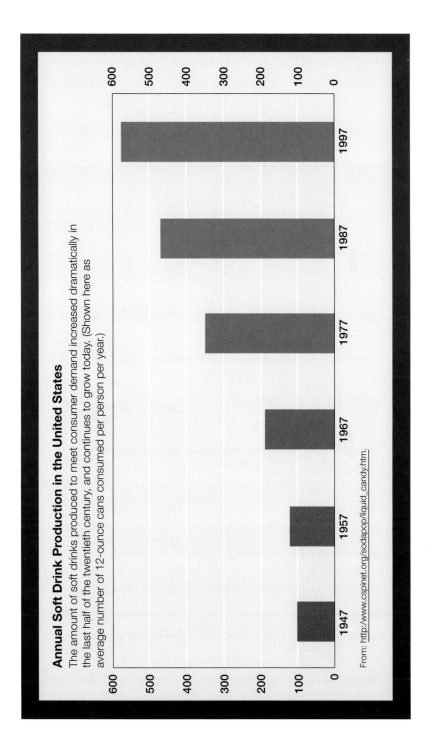

Annual Soft Drink Production in the United States

The amount of soft drinks produced to meet consumer demand increased dramatically in the last half of the twentieth century, and continues to grow today. (Shown here as average number of 12-ounce cans consumed per person per year.)

From: http://www.cspinet.org/sodapop/liquid_candy.htm.

35

very popular. By 2003 it was being shipped to millions of customers in more than a hundred countries.

Now there are dozens of energy drinks, with powered-up names such as Full Throttle, Rockstar, Monster, No Fear, and Guts. Many have caffeine added as a powder in the bottling or canning factory, plus guarana extract, which adds more caffeine. The total amount of caffeine is not stated on labels. Though the U.S. Food and Drug Administration put a limit of 6 mg per ounce on the amount of caffeine that can be legally added to beverages and foods, that limit does not apply to added foods such as guarana.

Billions of high-caffeine energy drinks are sold each year. Among their biggest fans are college students trying to study late, young hard-working people, fitness and exercise devotees, and dance club patrons seeking an energy high that lasts all night.

Some countries have banned these drinks, or are considering doing so. The main concern is that these drinks, with up to 400 mg of caffeine per can (counting the guarana), contain too much caffeine, especially since people often drink more than one can an evening. There have been a handful of cases in recent years of a person dying shortly after con-suming these beverages, though no evidence exists that caffeine was responsible for these deaths. For now, this warning is printed on the containers: "Not recommended for children, pregnant or breast-feeding women or caffeine-sensitive persons."

There are also bottled waters that have caffeine and/or guarana listed among the ingredients. Vending machines at schools sometimes offer these, apparently as an alternative to soft drinks. They don't usually have as high a sugar content as soft drinks, but the caffeine is there. Consumers must learn to read labels if they want to avoid—or consume—caffeine, as it shows up in some unlikely drinks.

Tea

Tea is another common source of caffeine in many cultures. It is important to realize that the word "tea" is used to mean many kinds of beverages made from some kind of plant material in hot (or sometimes cold) water. But the kinds of tea that contain caffeine are all derived from one plant species, *Camellia sinensis*, which is native to Southeast Asia. Camellia sinensis is an evergreen shrub that is cultivated in many tropical and sub-tropical areas of the world today, especially China, Tibet, Japan, Indonesia, India, Sri Lanka, Kenya, Turkey, and Argentina.

Tea is harvested by picking the leaves or leaf buds, then drying and heating them. Leaves heated the shortest time make green tea, which contains much of the plant's natural antioxidants. Some people prefer green tea to coffee because of the

Caffeine Content of Selected Soft Drinks

(Note: product manufacturers may have modified caffeine content since these values were obtained.)

12-OUNCE BEVERAGE	MILLI-GRAMS	12-OUNCE BEVERAGE	MILLI-GRAMS
Red Bull (8.2 oz)	80.0	Pepsi-Cola	37.5
Jolt	71.2	Coca-Cola Classic	34.0
Pepsi One	55.5	Canada Dry Cola	30.0
Mountain Dew	55.0	A&W Creme Soda	29.0
Kick Citrus	54.0		
Mellow Yellow	52.8	Barq's Root Beer	23.0
Surge	51.0	Canada Dry Diet Cola	1.2
Tab	46.8	Diet Rite Cola	0
Diet Coke	45.6	Sprite	0
Shasta Cola	44.4	7-Up	0
RC Cola	43.0	Mug Root Beer	0
Dr Pepper	41.0	Diet Barq's Root Beer	0
Mr. Pibb	40.0		
Sunkist Orange	40.0	A&W Root Beer	0
Ruby Red	39.0	Slice	0
Storm	38.0	Sierra Mist	0
Big Red	38.0	Fresca	0

Source: http://wilstar.com/caffeine.htm

Caffeine Content of Coffee and Tea

COFFEES	SERVING	CAFFEINE (MILLIGRAMS)
Coffee, brewed	8 ounces	40–180
Coffee, instant, plain	8 ounces	30–120
Coffee, instant, various flavored mixes	8 ounces	25–65
Coffee, espresso	2 ounces	100
Coffee, decaffeinated	8 ounces	1–5
TEAS		
Tea, black, leaf or bag	8 ounces	45–100
Tea, green, leaf or bag	8 ounces	20–30
Snapple Iced Tea, all varieties	16-ounce bottle	42
Lipton Iced Tea, assorted varieties	16-ounce bottle	18–40
Arizona Iced Tea, assorted varieties	16-ounce bottle	15–30
Celestial Seasonings Herbal Tea, all varieties	8 ounces	0

antioxidants in tea. Leaves that are left to dry for a few days start to darken, giving rise to "oolong" tea. Leaves that have dried for up to a month turn black and produce black tea (also called red tea because the color of the beverage is dark red). It takes approximately four pounds of fresh tea leaves to produce one pound of dried tea. Flavorings can be added to make special tea varieties. For example, Earl Grey tea has extracts of citrus fruit. Chai, a traditional tea from India, is a blend of strong black tea, milk, sweeteners, and spices.

The amount of caffeine in tea depends on how long it is brewed, with more caffeine seeping out of the leaves the longer they sit in hot water. Black tea contains about twice as much caffeine as green tea, probably because it is more thoroughly dried and shrunken, and takes more to fill a teabag. Tea also contains theobromine and theophylline, chemicals related to caffeine but with weaker stimulant effects. An average 8-ounce cup of tea contains about 50 mg of caffeine, 3 mg of theobromine, and 1 mg of theophylline.

Cola Nuts
Some foods and beverages include extracts from cola nuts, also referred to as kola, bissy, gooroo, or guru nuts. The trees from which they are harvested are native to West Africa, but are also grown nowadays in other warm, humid places such as South and Central America, the West Indies, India, Sri Lanka,

Southeast Asia, and China. The trees grow as tall as sixty feet. The fruits, which can be as long as eight inches, are green and rough-skinned with a white interior surrounding a bright red, flat seed (the "nut"). There are many species of cola trees, but *Cola anomala, Cola acuminata,* and *Cola nitida* are the most important as crops.

Cola nuts contain caffeine and a smaller amount of theobromine. They are used widely in Africa to make a beverage, but it is even more common to chew them. The nuts also hold a very important symbolic place in African culture, and are used in ceremonies, celebrations, business activities, prayers, and other cultural events.

Guarana
Guarana (sometimes called yoco) is a bushy tree that grows in the South American tropics, especially the Amazon River region of Brazil. Scientists are figuring out whether there are a few different kinds, or just one species of the plant. Currently three types are distinguished: *Paullinia cupana, Paullinia yoco,* and *Paullinia sorbilis.*

Indigenous tribes have long collected the orange-red fruit of guarana for its blackish seeds, which are roasted and peeled to expose an inner white material that is mixed with water to make a paste. That paste is formed into sticks, which are dried over a fire for about a month. Portions of the dry sticks are then grated into hot water to make a beverage. In addition, guarana is extremely popular in Brazil as a bottled soft drink, and is as common there as coffee (it was declared the "national beverage" in 1940).

Guarana seeds contain more caffeine than an equal weight of coffee beans, and also have some theophylline and theobromine. That makes them the richest known source of caffeinelike stimulants. Guarana is mostly cultivated on plantations in Brazil, and Brazil has been careful to keep this prized commodity from being cultivated outside the country. Today, the worldwide demand for guarana has become greater than the Brazilian plantations can provide, though the country is trying to increase its output.

Maté

Another popular beverage from South America is yerba maté (maté for short). It is made from the leaves of a shrub in the holly family. The leaves are dried (and sometimes toasted) and added to hot water, sometimes with spices, sweeteners, and/or milk. The indigenous people who drank maté long before it was bottled or put into tea bags, as it is today, drank it from a hollow gourd through a special straw that filtered out the plant material. Nowadays, people in South America still like to drink it from uniquely decorated silver or ceramic vessels using a silver straw.

There has been some confusion about whether maté contains caffeine or a different stimulant(s).

The name mateine has been used to refer to the stimulant in maté. It is described as different from caffeine—as a stereoisomer of caffeine. A stereoisomer refers to a molecule that is a mirror image of another molecule (like your left and right hands). And yet, the caffeine molecule doesn't have the kind of shape that would look any different in a mirror. So, mateine is really just another name for caffeine, but is sometimes used in advertising for maté products to (erroneously) suggest that mateine is an alternative to caffeine.

Still, yerba maté has other plant compounds and minerals that offer something beneficial. People

MATÉ IS A VERY POPULAR HOT CAFFEINATED BEVERAGE IN SOUTH AMERICA. MANY OF THOSE WHO DRINK IT FEEL IT CREATES THE GOOD EFFECTS OF COFFEE—FOR EXAMPLE, ALERTNESS—WITHOUT THE JITTERY SIDE EFFECTS.

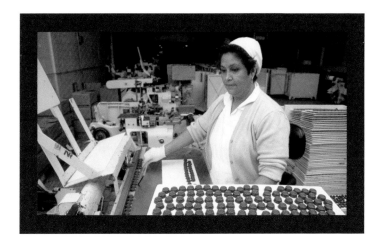

CHOCOLATE CONTAINS VERY LITTLE CAFFEINE, BUT SOMETIMES CAFFEINE IS ADDED.

who drink it say it doesn't cause the jitters, digestive turmoil, rapid heartbeat, or other unwanted side effects of coffee. That may be because it has much less caffeine (and a bit of theobromine), but people claim it works just as well as a stimulant. Whether it does—and how it would do so—is unclear.

Chocolate

Chocolate comes from the dried, fermented seeds of the cacao tree, *Theobroma cacao*. It is highly prized around the world and can be added to foods or beverages as the bitter powder of the ground seeds, or combined with sugar, milk, flavorings, and other ingredients to make confections, foods, or beverages. Three types of cacao are used to make chocolate products today, all of which grow in the New World tropics.

It is often said that chocolate contains caffeine, and it does—but only a small amount. It does have plenty of theobromine, but theobromine's stimulant effects are only about a seventh as strong as those of caffeine. It isn't clear whether theobromine can create dependence, as can caffeine. The word "chocoholic" is a playful term meaning someone who enjoys chocolate on a regular basis, and some people consider themselves chocoholics. But other substances in chocolate, such as sugar and fats, have a known pleasurable effect on the brain, which may be more important to a person's love of chocolate than the effects of theobromine.

Theobromine is toxic to many animals because they don't have the enzymes to break it down into inactive chemicals. Once in the animal's body, it stays around a long time and can cause heart attacks, seizures, internal bleeding, and death. Veterinarians warn people to *keep all forms of chocolate away from animals.*

Foods

Coffee-flavored ice cream and yogurt contain caffeine. The amount varies dramatically, from a few milligrams per serving to the amount in a soft drink, and occasionally more. The amounts are not listed on the product, but can be found by calling or writing the manufacturer or looking on the Internet.

Some foods called energy bars contain caffeine, guarana, green tea, or cola nut (kola, bissy, gooroo, or guru)—or combinations of these. The first type of

Caffeine Content of Selected Foods

(Note: product manufacturers may have modified caffeine content since these values were obtained.)

FROZEN DESSERTS	SERVING	CAFFEINE (MG)
Ben & Jerry's No Fat Coffee Fudge Frozen Yogurt	1 cup	85
Starbucks Coffee Ice Cream	1 cup	40–60
Häagen-Dazs Coffee Ice Cream	1 cup	58
Häagen-Dazs Coffee Frozen Yogurt, fat-free	1 cup	40
YOGURTS		
Dannon Coffee	8 ounces	45
Yoplait Café Au Lait	6 ounces	5
Dannon Light Cappuccino	8 ounces	<1
Stonyfield Farm Cappuccino	8 ounces	0
CHOCOLATES		
Chocolate milk	8 ounces	4
Cocoa or hot chocolate	8 ounces	4–10
Dark chocolate bar	1 ounce	20–25
Milk chocolate bar	1 ounce	3–6

Sources:
Center for Science in the Public Interest (www.cspinet.org/new/caffeine.htm)
About.com online (coffeetea.about.com/library/blcaffeine.htm)
McKinley Health Center (www.mckinley.uiuc.edu/health-info/drug-alc/caffeine.html)
Weinberg and Bealer, 2001, p. 327-329

energy bar, PowerBar, which was created by marathon runner Brian Maxwell in the 1980s, was formulated to provide concentrated, energy-rich food and nutrients. It had no caffeine. But now some energy bars give the kick of caffeine—and some give a lot. Energy gels, which are edible, sometimes contain caffeine. These gels come in single serving packets, meant to give a speedy energy boost, especially during exercise.

Pills and Medicines
Purified caffeine is available in pills known as "alertness aids." NoDoz and Vivarin are two popular brands, and there are several others. They typically contain 100 mg of caffeine each, about the same amount as a cup of coffee. People choose these pills when they aren't interested in consuming a beverage, or when it's inconvenient to drink one or difficult to find one, such as on long drives late at night when restaurants are closed.

Caffeine also is included in some pain relievers. Although it isn't certain just how caffeine helps to tame pain, it has become a standard ingredient in some brands of pain relievers containing aspirin or acetaminophen. Caffeine also is part of some medicines that help prevent migraine headaches if taken as soon as symptoms begin. Some antihistamine medicines, which reduce allergy symptoms, can make a person drowsy, so caffeine is added to some of them to counteract the sleepiness.

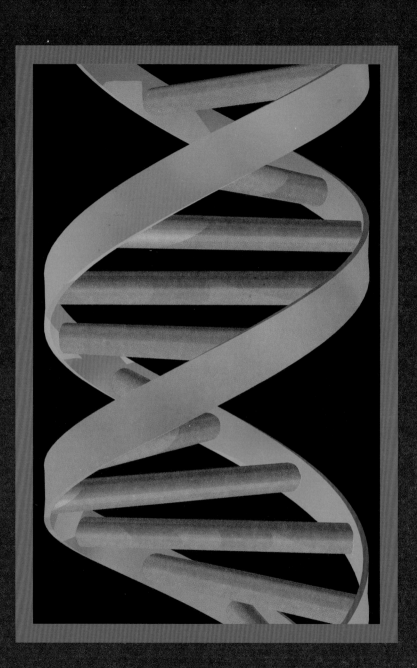

PURINE, A VERY IMPORTANT PART OF EACH MOLECULE OF CAFFEINE, IS PART OF WHAT MAKES UP DNA, WHICH IS SHOWN HERE.

3 CAFFEINE AND THE METHYLXANTHINES

Just what is caffeine? It is a fairly simple molecule consisting of carbon (C), hydrogen (H), nitrogen (N), and oxygen (O) atoms. Its chemical formula is $C_8H_{10}N_4O_2$ (each small number after a letter represents how many of that particular atom are in a single caffeine molecule). Among chemists, caffeine has other names that reveal something about it. One is 3,7-dihydro-1,3,7-trimethyl-1H-purine-2,6-dione. That is a very long and cumbersome name, but an important part is the word *purine*. A purine is a particular arrangement of carbon, hydrogen, and nitrogen atoms that looks like two rings side by side. It forms a part of each caffeine molecule.

Purine is found in some very important molecules within living organisms, including people. One is DNA (deoxyribonucleic acid), the material that encodes the genetic information passed on from generation to generation. DNA is composed of millions of purine-containing molecules (as well as other types of chemical structures). RNA (ribonucleic acid) has a structure similar to that of DNA, so it has purines, too. RNA has a diversity of functions that are essential to life. A molecule that contains just one purine is ATP (adenosine triphosphate), an energy-containing chemical upon which all our cells rely.

PICTURED HERE IS A PHOTOMICROGRAPH OF PURIFIED CAFFEINE CRYSTALS.

Another name for caffeine is 1,3,7-trimethylxan-thine. A chemist would recognize that the –*xanthine* portion (pronounced "zantheen") means that the purine part of caffeine actually has two oxygen atoms attached to it. Then there is the *methyl* por-tion of the name. That's shorthand for a cluster of atoms consisting of a carbon with three hydrogens attached to it. Caffeine has three methyls attached to the xanthine structure (hence, the *trimethyl* in the name. The numbers stand for where the methyls are attached to the xanthine).

So, caffeine can be referred to as a methylxan-thine. The reason this is important is that there are other methylxanthines: theophylline and theo-bromine, which differ from caffeine in that they only have two methyl groups each. They are some-times present in the same plants that contain caf-feine. For example, tea leaves contain caffeine, theobromine, and theophylline. Some descriptions of tea emphasize its theophylline content, as though it were the main chemical responsible for tea's stimulating effects. And though theophylline is indeed a stimulant, the amount in tea is very small compared to its caffeine content. There is also only a small amount of theobromine in tea.

Chocolate is often said to contain caffeine. And yet only a tiny amount is present in the edible por-tion of cacao pods, from which chocolate foods and beverages are made. Cacao (and chocolate) does, however, contain theobromine—about 1.3 percent of the weight of pure cacao. Theobromine is a much weaker stimulant than caffeine. However, some chocolate products have additional caffeine put in, and sometimes it's quite a lot.

It is interesting that theophylline and theobromine are both *metabolites* of caffeine. That means that, once inside the body, some of the caffeine is converted into these other molecules. Eventually, they are all converted into other molecules that have no stimulating effect and are cleared from the body in urine.

From Beverage to Bloodstream
Caffeine is easily absorbed into the bloodstream from the digestive tract. It then is carried with the blood to all parts of the body, and easily moves out of blood vessels and into cells. Within half an hour to an hour of drinking a cup of coffee or other caffeinated beverage, caffeine reaches its highest concentration in the blood, so it will have the most noticeable influence then. If food has been consumed at the same time, it will take a little longer for all the caffeine to get into the bloodstream.

Caffeine has an influence on cells in the body as long as it is being carried to them in the bloodstream. But when caffeine passes into liver cells, enzymes change its structure. About a dozen different molecules are made from it, called caffeine *metabolites*. They include the other methylxanthines, theophylline and theobromine, and paraxanthine (very similar but without any methyl groups).

These can get back into the bloodstream, where they continue to travel around and have a stimulant effect on cells.

It takes hours for the kidneys (which make the urine) to clear caffeine from the blood. Scientists have done experiments in which volunteers were given a known amount of caffeine, after which samples of their blood were taken every few hours. It was discovered that half of the caffeine was gone from the bloodstream in about four hours, while a small amount still lingered twelve to fifteen hours later. But each person gets rid of the caffeine at a different rate. How long it takes depends on many things, including a person's age, health, whether other drugs are present in the bloodstream, and genetics (which can determine how well the enzymes in the liver work to metabolize caffeine).

For example, smoking cigarettes speeds up caffeine metabolism and removes its stimulating effects faster. (That may be why people who smoke and drink coffee at the same time tend to drink more coffee than people who don't smoke.) On the other hand, someone who has liver damage may have problems breaking down the caffeine into inactive metabolites, so its stimulating effects last longer. Caffeine metabolism is also slower in women who are taking oral birth control pills or who are pregnant.

Compared to adults, children and especially infants metabolize caffeine very slowly. Toddlers require about four times longer to rid their systems of it, and infants twenty times longer. It may seem unlikely that toddlers and infants would consume caffeine, but it can be in foods, beverages, and medicines they might be given. In addition, caffeine is passed to nursing infants in breast milk.

Caffeine Meets Cells
Before caffeine is inactivated by the liver and removed by the kidneys, it has a variety of effects on cells. Of particular interest to researchers is what it does to make people feel more alert and energized. The most likely explanation is that caffeine prevents a naturally occurring molecule, adenosine, from attaching to brain cells and other nerve cells throughout the body (also called neurons). Adenosine's overall action appears to be slowing down brain activity. The amount of adenosine in the brain increases the longer a person is awake and active. It is something like a natural rest inducer because as it accumulates, it has a greater action on quieting down brain activity, making a person drowsy and fatigued.

Caffeine gets in the way of adenosine by attaching to places on neurons where adenosine would have if caffeine hadn't gotten there first. It probably can do so because adenosine and caffeine both contain a purine structure. By blocking some of the adenosine, caffeine interferes with the opportunity for brain neurons (and possibly neurons elsewhere) to rest. One way to understand this is to compare brain activity to the speed of a car. The gas pedal will speed the car up, and the brakes will slow it down. Adenosine is like the brakes. But caffeine is not like the gas pedal—instead, it prevents the brakes from being used as much.

In addition to enhancing brain activity, caffeine mimics some aspects of a person's natural stress response. That response is normally triggered by chemicals released by the adrenal gland called epinephrine or norepinephrine (or adrenaline and noradrenaline). The response includes a temporary increase in breathing, heart rate, and blood pressure, and causes sweating and shakiness—all of which caffeine also can cause.

Caffeine does some other interesting things to cells. For example, laboratory experiments of individual cells show that it influences where the cells store calcium. Caffeine enhances a nerve cell's ability to use calcium in such a way that it sends messages faster to other cells. Caffeine allows muscle cells to use calcium to make them contract more strongly and/or rapidly. That includes muscles of the digestive tract and of the heart. Calcium also increases the number of dendritic spines on neurons. The spines stick out from a neuron toward others and allow it to receive signals from them. Researchers wonder if calcium might be creating more dendritic spines in the brains of people who consume caffeine, thus improving neuron communication and brain function. Fascinating though this

Caffeine Helps Study Epilepsy

Caffeine is proving helpful in research about diseases that have nothing to do with caffeine consumption. One example is the study of epilepsy. Epilepsy is a disorder in which neurons in the brain suddenly become active, sending signals at random to the rest of the body. That causes, among other things, a temporary but very intense contraction of muscles known as a seizure. Although it is not entirely clear why the brain sends out sudden bursts of signals that cause a seizure, one thing researchers do know is that neurons must use calcium to do so. Calcium is present inside neurons, and gets moved to different places within them when the neurons are sending signals. It also has been discovered, from studies of neurons from the brains of animals (it's hard to do work on human brains), that caffeine placed inside neurons makes calcium movement greater, and makes the neurons more active in sending signals. The useful part of this discovery is that drugs might be created to block that calcium movement. Caffeine is being used in experiments of such drugs. The caffeine causes calcium movement, and various drugs can be tested for their ability to reduce or prevent that movement.

is, the amount of caffeine used in these laboratory experiments is higher than beverages or even caffeine pills could safely provide.

Another of caffeine's effects is to stimulate the body's usage of stored fats for energy, while lowering its usage of sugars. This, combined with caffeine's overall boost to brain activity, is why caffeine is included in many weight-loss products.

Caffeine is also said to be a diuretic—to cause excess loss of body water in urine by altering kidney function. And though this is commonly mentioned as a downside of caffeine consumption, newer evidence suggests that it doesn't generate any more urine than the amount of fluid that was in the beverage itself.

There are yet other ways caffeine interacts with cells, and surely many more will be discovered. Just how caffeine's influence on individual cells translates into changes in a whole person's physiology isn't always clear. But caffeine does have some proven benefits and some possible health dangers.

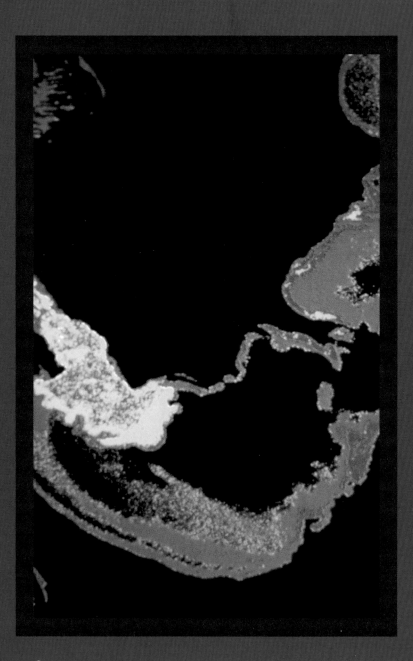

SOME PEOPLE WHO DRINK COFFEE EXPERIENCE HEARTBURN, A PAINFUL IRRITATION WHERE THE ESOPHAGUS MEETS THE STOMACH. THE YELLOW IN THIS THERMOGRAPH SHOWS INCREASED BLOOD FLOW IN THE IRRITATED AREA.

4 CAFFEINE'S EFFECTS ON THE BODY

A variety of studies conducted over several decades have shown that caffeine helps people stay awake (sometimes longer than they want to), enhances performance on mental tasks, improves hand–eye coordination, speeds up reaction time, and boosts energy for muscular work, including sports and exercise. (Caffeine does *not* counteract alcohol's effects, even though an intoxicated person might feel more awake!) Caffeine also confers a sense of well being or lifted mood in many people.

On the other hand, there has been a lot of concern that caffeine might be dangerous to a person's health because many people consume it on a daily basis for decades. Plus, studies from the 1950s and

1970s showed that high doses of caffeine could damage DNA in *plants* and some people worried that it could damage *their* DNA.

This chapter summarizes what conclusions are most reasonable at this time about the good and bad influences of caffeine on health. These conclusions come from many scientific studies, but it is important to note that not everyone agrees on what the findings mean. Studies rarely give black and white answers if conducted on real people out in the real world—as most caffeine studies have been. In addition, it can be difficult to compare one study to another to be sure the findings are accurate, since the factors that are being considered are often different, and the people studied represent different subsets of the population. For example, one study might compare the number of caffeinated beverages consumed daily by male athletes to see how it influences their blood pressure, while another study might compare caffeine consumption and blood pressure among average people or overweight people.

Another difficulty with studies of caffeine's influence on health is that many are based on indirect evidence. Such a study might divide a group of volunteers into subsets based on the number of caffeinated beverages they drink daily (for example, those who drink none, those who drink three cups or fewer, and those who drink more than three cups), and then look for the types of ailments that are most common in each group. These kinds of studies do their best to account for all other variables, such as a person's age or whether he or she smokes, before concluding that ailments that are more common in people who consume a lot of caffeine are indeed related to the caffeine rather than another cause. Still other studies interview people who already have a specific health problem, such as cancer or kidney disease, and ask how much caffeine they have been consuming.

It is especially important to recognize that most studies have looked at the influence of caffeinated *beverages* on people, not caffeine itself. Also, the amount of caffeine in those beverages was not measured, and surely would have varied widely. Many researchers admit that their findings of health problems may be due to other substances in the beverages. For example, some coffee drinkers get heartburn, a sensation of pain around the stomach area caused by stomach acid coming in contact with the lower part of the esophagus (the tube that carries food into the stomach). Caffeine does enhance digestion, but heartburn has not been convincingly blamed on caffeine, and may be caused by other substances in coffee.

Alertness and Task Performance
There is clear evidence from scientific studies that caffeine helps people stay alert, and many people have figured that out from personal experience. It is no coincidence that caffeinated beverages and alertness aids are used by truck drivers, emergency

workers, late-night shift workers, military person-nel, and other people who have to keep focused on a task for a long time without taking a rest. Because of this, caffeine has been praised by some as a drug that may have saved thousands of lives.

MILITARY PERSONNEL OFTEN FIND CAFFEINE AN INVALUABLE AID IN STAYING ALERT WHEN SLEEP IS NOT AN OPTION.

Military Pilots Get a Boost

The U.S. Air Force Office of Scientific Research funded a study on the effects of caffeine on alertness. Researchers at Harvard Medical School and Brigham and Women's Hospital in Boston studied sixteen healthy men kept awake for twenty-eight hours and asleep for fourteen, over the course of twenty-nine days. This made them stay awake longer than most people would, and they often were awake at night, and sometimes asleep during the day. Half the men took caffeine tablets every hour while awake, and the other half didn't. Several tests of their mental awareness and abilities showed that caffeine helped the men to stay alert and think clearly in spite of this very odd schedule.

The researchers concluded that caffeine can help people perform jobs that take longer than the usual awake period of most people (sixteen hours). The study's lead researcher, James Wyatt, Ph.D., also realized that caffeine would be most helpful if taken later in the day—something that many people avoid because they fear they won't sleep well. "I hate to say it," said Wyatt, "but most of the population is using caffeine the wrong way by drinking a few mugs of coffee or tea in the morning."

Studies also show that caffeine helps people concentrate longer and do better on simple mental or physical tasks. But an interesting outcome of studies was the finding that caffeine helped people do simple and familiar tasks faster and more accurately, but had the opposite effect on new tasks: they did worse. Researchers explain these observations by proposing that caffeine gives a boost of energy that helps a person do routine things, but that same energy makes it harder to settle down and patiently tackle a complex or new mental challenge.

Some studies show that caffeine doesn't improve how well a person does things when she or he *already* feels awake and energized. Instead, it has its most noticeable effects after boredom, fatigue, or a hypnotic state has already set in, as can happen when doing a repetitive task over and over (including driving on a highway for a long time). There is also evidence from studies that caffeine isn't any better at overcoming fatigue than is taking a break to get up and move around.

Mood

People say things like, "If I wake up feeling kind of depressed, a cup of coffee can turn that around." That change in mood is often attributed to caffeine.

Studies have shown that people who consume caffeine are less likely to be depressed. One study of more than 86,000 female nurses by a researcher at Harvard Medical School looked for a relationship between caffeine consumption and suicide. Nurses who drank two or more cups of coffee a day were less likely to become depressed enough to commit suicide than non-coffee drinkers. Another study of nearly 130,000 men and women found the same thing. (Studies of this size haven't been carried out for tea or soda.)

The researchers of those studies are not, however, urging people to go out and start drinking coffee to thwart depression, because there could be several other explanations for the results. The habit of taking time to enjoy *any* beverage might help. Or stopping by a local café might provide a sense of community. Or maybe other substances, such as added sugar, provide an energy boost or alter other mood-influencing chemicals in the brain.

Nevertheless, the ability to fight fatigue for a while, which caffeine does, might have a ripple effect that improves a person's mood.

Sports Performance

Scientists and sports experts mostly agree that caffeine helps with endurance sports such as swimming, cycling, and tennis. In general, athletes involved in endurance sports fare better with some caffeine in their systems. However, caffeine does not appear to help with short-term sports, such as sprinting, which require bursts of activity.

An explanation for why caffeine improves endurance but not short-term abilities has to do with the energy supply—the "fuel"—that muscle cells use

Are Athletes Who Use Caffeine Cheating?

Until 2003, caffeine had been on the list of drugs banned for international athletes, including those competing in the Olympic games. Because of its overall stimulatory and energy-boosting effect, taking a lot of caffeine before a competition was considered a deliberate attempt to have an unfair advantage. The amount that would get an athlete disqualified had been the equivalent of drinking about ten average 8-ounce cups of coffee—about 1,000 mg, usually taken in tablet form.

Inger Miller, an American who had won a bronze in the 60-meter sprint at the 1999 World Indoor Championships, and Letitia Vriesde, of Surinam, who had won a gold medal for the 800-meter run at the Pan American Games in August 2003, lost their medals because they tested positive for caffeine.

Some sports experts offer suggestions to athletes about when and how much caffeine to take for best results. For example, they say, don't have any caffeine for the few days before a competition. That will make its effects stronger when it is taken, preferably three to four hours before a competition. Is this fair? Athletic competitions are full of controversy about what competitors do to win. Caffeine seems a humble drug compared to anabolic steroids, erythropoietin (EPO), prescription, and other illegal stimulants, but it, too, *is* a drug.

during exercise. The cells can use both fats and glucose. Glucose is a very important sugar made by the body, and it is also present in carbohydrates. Glucose is stored in muscle and other cells as a larger molecule, glycogen. Working muscles usually use their glycogen supplies first, then shift to using fats from the bloodstream when the glycogen starts running out. Caffeine, however, shifts this pattern. It causes muscle cells to start using fats after about fifteen minutes of exercise. That means that muscles can draw on both glycogen and fats for fuel if exercise continues longer. Eventually, the muscles will tire, but this dual fuel supply allows them to work longer first.

Caffeine's effects on athletes vary, depending on factors such as how often the person consumes caffeine, what foods were recently eaten and how much, what other types of stimulants are in the bloodstream, and how good the person's liver is at metabolizing caffeine into inactive metabolites. Sports aficionados describe how and when to take caffeine for the best performance results, but some people react to caffeine with abdominal cramps and diarrhea. Needless to say, that could get in the way of a good sports performance.

Weight Loss

Caffeine is included in a variety of weight-loss products, for several reasons. First, it has no calories on its own (though sugar-laden soft drinks or coffee drinks containing milk, sugar, and chocolate can add hundreds of calories per beverage). Second, caffeine increases the body's production of epinephrine and norepinephrine. These chemicals are naturally released during times when energy is needed to be physically active and alert, and they dampen sensations of hunger. Third, caffeine influences the way the body fuels itself. Specifically, it helps to get fats out of storage and into the bloodstream, where they can be used for energy instead of contributing to a person's girth.

People do report losing weight on caffeine-containing products. However, caffeine can undermine weight loss. As it makes a person more energetic, his or her body uses up more of its stored fats and glucose. Those responses trigger a sensation of hunger. Caffeine also stirs up digestive activity, which acts both as a psychological and physiological reminder of food.

Another reason caffeine may not work as a weight-loss drug is that when its effects wear off, people can experience a "crash," or energy low. If they cannot take a nap, they may choose a high-calorie snack instead.

Diabetes Mellitus
Caffeine appears to stimulate the pancreas to release more insulin into the bloodstream than usual. Insulin is a very important hormone, a release of which is triggered by digested foods from a meal as they enter the bloodstream, as well as by other

hormones. One of insulin's most important activities is to encourage cells to take in sugars, fats, and amino acids from the bloodstream. Diabetes mellitus is a condition in which the pancreas does not produce enough, or any, insulin. That causes abnormal usage of energy molecules by the body and that, in turn, can damage blood vessels, the heart, and other organs. There are two types of diabetes mellitus, Type 1 and Type 2. A person with Type 1 diabetes mellitus lacks the cells in the pancreas that would make insulin because the body's immune system malfunctions and destroys the person's own pancreas cells. This usually affects children, and is sometimes referred to as juvenile-onset diabetes.

A person with Type 2 diabetes mellitus has a pancreas that is capable of producing insulin, but that does not make enough. This low insulin production is usually due to overeating for years. It appears that too much food intake over time makes the pancreas less able to make the right amount of insulin. People with Type 2 diabetes often can bring their insulin production back to a more normal level by reducing food intake and increasing exercise. However, they usually need to take medicines to help improve their condition.

Caffeine may have some influence on a person's likelihood of developing Type 2 diabetes mellitus. In Finland (where more coffee is consumed per person than in any other country) a ten-year study of nearly 15,000 men and women found that those who drank three or four cups of coffee a day were less likely to develop Type 2 diabetes mellitus than people who drank no coffee. Tea also had this protective effect. Still, the researchers felt that caffeine's influence might be small or unimportant compared to the many other substances in the beverages. Clearly, this needs further study, especially since different findings by other researchers has led to the recommendation that people who have Type 2 diabetes mellitus avoid caffeine, at least at mealtimes.

Heart Disease
Although caffeine affects the cardiovascular system (heart and blood vessels) while it is in someone's bloodstream, there is no convincing evidence that it causes heart disease over years of moderate consumption (health experts say that means less than 300 mg a day). Caffeine does increase heart rate, narrow the diameter of blood vessels, and elevate blood pressure. These are short-term changes that appear not to cause long-term problems. The Framingham Heart Study was an especially large study that looked for increases in heart attacks and strokes related to caffeine use, and found none.

Asthma and Apnea
Asthma is an increasingly common lung disorder in which the tubes that bring air into the lungs (especially the small ones known as bronchioles)

become temporarily narrowed, making it hard for air to move in and out. The methylxanthines are sometimes used in pill form or by injection (in an emergency) to treat asthma or other lung diseases in which breathing is difficult. Caffeine and theophylline (and another methylxanthine, aminophylline), counteract this by causing muscles that ring the bronchioles to relax, allowing the tubes to open wider. Different drugs that can be inhaled directly into the lungs are a more common treatment of asthma nowadays, however.

A doctor may also use methylxanthines (especially theophylline), given by injection, to treat premature infants with a condition called preterm apnea, in which they go for many seconds without breathing. Theophylline has been used to keep these babies breathing, but too much of it can cause rapid heartbeat, seizures, or other problems. Caffeine is being evaluated by doctors as a better alternative because it seems just as effective, and works at doses that are not as likely to cause a racing heartbeat as do effective doses of theophylline. Doctors must be very cautious about how much they give of either drug, however, because infants clear methylxanthines from the blood very slowly.

Caffeine Sensitivity or Overdose
Caffeine has some adverse effects. It can cause "jitters"—shakiness, nervousness, and difficulty concentrating or staying calm. The amount of caffeine it takes to cause jitters depends on the person.

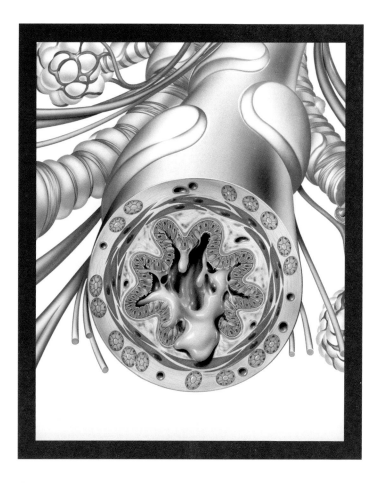

THIS ARTWORK DEPICTS THE WAY A BRONCHIOLE OF A PERSON WITH ASTHMA LOOKS DURING AN ATTACK.

Some people are naturally very sensitive to caffeine and react to just one beverage. Other people consume several cups daily and don't feel jittery, though they might if they were to have more than their usual amount. A person's reaction to caffeine is influenced by other factors, such as the amount of food in the stomach (food slows the absorption of caffeine into the bloodstream) and how recently the person has had other caffeine-containing drinks, foods, or medications.

Caffeine can also cause adverse reactions that are more serious than the jitters. Problems can include dizziness, rapid and pounding heartbeat, extreme restlessness, anxiety, digestive turmoil (cramps, diarrhea, nausea, vomiting), confusion, and even seizures. There is no specific amount of caffeine that is certain to cause these reactions because everyone is different. Similarly, it isn't possible to define an amount that would constitute an "overdose." In rare instances, people have died of caffeine overconsumption, but that was from taking thousands of milligrams at once, in the form of caffeine pills (which have 100 mg or 200 mg each).

Consumers need to be aware that the possibility of having unpleasant reactions to caffeine can happen unexpectedly because the amount of caffeine in many beverages and foods usually isn't written on the label. It is helpful to recognize the names of caffeine-containing ingredients because the more of them there are, the higher the caffeine content is likely to be. Green tea, guarana, yerba maté, maté, cola, kola, bissy, guru, and gooroo—these all contain caffeine. Some products describe guarana as the "herbal form of caffeine," but caffeine is a molecule that comes in only one form, regardless of the source.

Cancer

Many studies have investigated a possible relationship between urinary bladder cancer and coffee. The worry is that urine is stored in the bladder for hours and would expose bladder cells to caffeine and/or its metabolites that are removed from the bloodstream by the kidneys. While there is a suggestion in some studies that bladder cancer happens more often in coffee drinkers, none have revealed a clear link.

A large study in 1981 showed that coffee drinkers had a higher likelihood of getting pancreatic cancer, but a review by scientists of dozens of studies since then has not come to the same conclusion. For other types of cancer, studies provide no clear cause for concern that coffee drinking increases risk.

Several studies have found a relationship between the amount of coffee a person drinks and the likelihood that he or she will get liver cancer, liver cirrhosis (an irreversible destruction of liver cells), or gallstones (hard nodules that form within the gall bladder, an organ situated within the liver that concentrates a digestion-aiding substance called bile). The relationship is not, however, that coffee is bad for the liver or gall bladder. Instead, those studies found that people who consumed coffee were *less* likely to have problems with their liver and with gallstones than people who didn't.

An example of one of those studies is from Japan, in which the health of more than 90,000 people was observed for ten years. Over that time, the number of people who got liver cancer was nearly three times higher among those who almost never drank coffee than among those who did. What's more, people who drank the most coffee each day were the least likely to get cancer.

There is also evidence that caffeinated coffee (but not decaffeinated, or tea) lowers a person's risk of getting colon cancer. That's what a group of scientists concluded when they reviewed seventeen different studies on the topic.

While these are interesting findings about coffee as a possible protector against liver disease, gallstones, and some forms of cancer, it is not clear whether this is due to the caffeine or to other substances in the coffee bean—and there are many. It is true that caffeine influences how the body uses fats, and liver disease can include the accumulation of fat in that organ. Caffeine also increases movement of foods and waste through the digestive tract, which might reduce accumulation of cancer-related irritants there. But much more work needs to be done before caffeine itself can be shown as protective.

There have been a handful of studies linking maté with cancer of the mouth and upper digestive tract. In one, people who drank large amounts of maté regularly were ten times more likely to develop cancer of the esophagus than people who drank none. Another study found the rate of cancer of the larynx to be three times higher among maté drinkers. These associations between maté and

75

cancer might be caused by the frequent drinking of extremely hot liquid (maté often is near boiling when consumed), and the damage that inflicts on the lining of the mouth and throat, or substances in the maté besides caffeine.

Osteoporosis and Bone Health

An example of the confusion between the effects of caffeine and those of caffeine-containing beverages comes up when talking about bone health. Headlines in magazines or on the Internet will say something like "Caffeine is bad for your bones," but then reveal that the basis for the headline was a study of caffeinated beverages. The Framingham Heart Study discovered that people who drank coffee over several years suffered hip fractures more often than people who didn't drink it. That's bad, but many people then interpret this to mean that caffeine is probably interfering with calcium accumulation in bones. Even lengthy review papers on the topic interchange the word "caffeine" for "coffee" or "caffeine-containing beverages."

Coffee contains many other plant compounds that might directly or indirectly influence a person's bone health. Sodas typically contain a lot of phosphorous. Some studies show that high levels of phosphorus consumption without an increase in calcium intake may disrupt the balance of those two components in bones, and cause calcium to be lost from bones into the bloodstream. (Other studies contradict this, as the soft drink industry is quick to point out.) And one study found that tea drinkers had *stronger* bones than people who did not drink tea. Another complication in ferreting out caffeine's effects from the beverages it comes in is that, more and more, people are choosing to drink soda (with its excessive phosphorus) instead of milk (with its calcium).

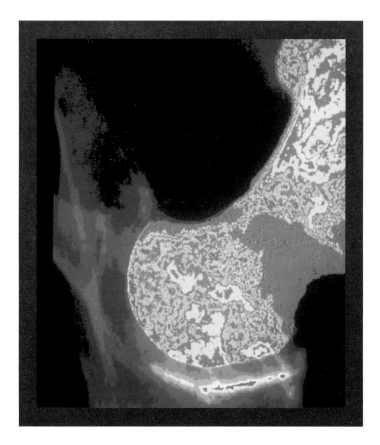

THIS X-RAY SHOWS A THIGH BONE AFFECTED BY OSTEOPOROSIS.

CAFFEINE HAS BEEN SHOWN TO HAVE AN EFFECT ON FETUSES AND BABIES WHO
ARE BREASTFED.

Although opinions strongly differ on this topic, the unresolved question of coffee's (and soft drinks') influence on bones may be a good reason to keep consumption low.

Pregnancy and Breastfeeding

Caffeine can be passed to a woman's developing fetus, across the placenta. Not only is the fetus very small, so that only a small amount of caffeine might affect its development, but fetal metabolism of caffeine is extremely slow. That means caffeine would last longer in the bloodstream and could cause problems with heart rhythm. Miscarriages and a lower birth weight of newborns have been associated with caffeine intake of over 300 mg a day by the mother. Also, caffeine gets into breast milk and some babies appear to have trouble sleeping and are abnormally restless or irritable when their mothers have had more than a couple of caffeinated beverages a day.

Because of these findings, the U.S. Food and Drug Administration (FDA) officially recommends that women who are pregnant or nursing keep their caffeine intake low.

Caffeine's Companions

There is another concern to mention regarding caffeinated beverages and foods: they typically come along with other ingredients that can be a problem to someone's health. Sodas are little more than highly sweetened, artificially flavored and colored fizzy water with added caffeine—and they are thought to contribute to a person's chances of becoming obese. Sugar-free versions contain artificial sweeteners, and therefore have no calories. But some physicians and health experts warn that artificial sweeteners, and synthetic dyes and flavorings, are not the safe chemicals we assume they are. Some people are allergic to these additives, and artificial sweeteners are suspected by some physicians to trigger headaches, vision problems, dizziness, seizures, and other reactions. Other caffeinated beverages, such as specialty coffee and tea drinks, are a concoction of milk products, sugar, artificial flavors and colorings, and a lot of calories.

People who drink a lot of coffee often also smoke tobacco. Smoking carries very well-established health risks. Plus, heavy smokers clear caffeine from their bloodstream twice as fast as nonsmokers, and they will consume more coffee to compensate for that.

Summary
A good summary of caffeine's effects on health is that it can be useful, and even help save lives by keeping people alert in emergency or dangerous situations. It can help a person be more productive in some tasks, although it can also interfere with concentration, and doesn't replace sleep.

Caffeine has some side effects that cause short-term problems, but these, and any long-term effects, don't appear to pose a serious health danger to most people if consumption is kept below about 300 mg a day. An exception might be among young people, in whom it takes longer to clear caffeine from the bloodstream than it does in adults. Plus, their caffeine consumption has been increasing over the years, as carbonated beverages work their way into nearly every youth-oriented social activity.

Finally, much more needs to be clarified to separate the effects of caffeine and the beverages in which it may be only one of many ingredients.

TO DECAF OR NOT TO DECAF? SOMETIMES, WE HAVE TO FIGHT OUR DESIRES IN FAVOR OF OUR HEALTH.

5 GETTING OFF CAFFEINE

Are the effects of caffeine worth being con-cerned about? Compared to other drugs that are both addictive and potentially very dangerous, such as heroin or alcohol, caffeine is virtually harmless.

One recurring concern, however, is its habit-forming nature. Does it create dependence? And if so, does that mean some effort should be made to reduce its consumption? Psychologists Laura Juliano and Roland Griffiths wrote in *Psychiatric Times* magazine that caffeine presents no serious threats to society. They do point out, however, that caffeine is consumed by hundreds of millions of people each day in amounts that really do influence behavior by changing brain chemistry. There is enough evidence that a psychological or physical need for caffeine develops among people who consume it that caffeine is discussed in an important book used by psychiatrists and therapists —*The Diagnostic and Statistical Manual of Mental Disorders IV (DSM-IV)*. The book summarizes a wide variety of mental and emotional problems from which people suffer. It includes four problems that caffeine can cause for people: caffeine intoxication (overdose), caffeine-induced anxiety disorder, caffeine-induced sleep disorder, and caffeine dependence syndrome.

Caffeine Dependence and Withdrawal

Many people say they are "addicted" to having their daily dose(s) of caffeinated beverages or foods. What does being addicted actually mean? As it turns out, it is a very complex issue. The definition has been used in the past to mean a physical need for a substance, such that unpleasant physical symptoms result when it isn't consumed. Experiencing those unpleasant symptoms is called withdrawal. However, doctors and psychologists today prefer the term *dependence* over addiction, and distinguish between physical and psychological dependence. *Physical* dependence refers to the body's need for a substance, such that withdrawal results when use of the substance is suddenly interrupted. *Psychological* dependence means a person feels a longing or desire for a substance when he or she stops taking it, but has no physical reactions. But a person who has strong emotional reactions and mood changes when going without that substance may be consid-

84

ered by some psychologists to be going through a form of withdrawal.

A guideline psychologists use to determine whether someone is dependent on a substance is to ask three questions: Does the person use the substance out of a sense of craving, longing, or need? Does the person feel that he or she can't really control the desire to use it? And does she or he continue using the substance in spite of known ill effects of doing so?

CHOOSING TO KICK CAFFEINE CAN BE DIFFICULT. ONE PROVEN WAY TO FIND ENERGY ASIDE FROM CAFFEINE IS EXERCISE.

A yes to those three questions regarding caf-feinated beverages suggests dependence. But dependence on what? It could be: to the caffeine itself; to the beverage, food, or medicine containing it; to the pleasure of consuming it in a certain setting, at a certain time, or with certain people. Most likely it will be a combination of these. People may say yes to the first two questions, but not be sure about the last because little evidence exists of any serious ill effects of caffeine when ingested in moderate amounts.

Psychiatrists can use a longer list of questions to help them decide if a person is dependent on a substance. The questions include whether a person experiences withdrawal or tolerance, which indicate addiction. Tolerance means that the person needs to consume more and more of the substance over time to get the same feeling that less of it used to create.

In the largest of studies that looked at whether caffeine users were dependent, about a third of the people were considered so by researchers because they met three or four of the list's seven criteria. The most common sign of dependence mentioned was the inability to use less even if desired. Teenagers aren't often included in studies of caffeine, but one study looked for dependence specifically in teenagers, and found that a fifth of them fit the criteria.

The Decaffeination Process

The most common method of removing caffeine from coffee involves soaking green coffee beans in hot water for several hours, which leeches out the caffeine. It may take several soakings to get most of the caffeine out (decaffeinated coffee is allowed by law to retain up to 3 percent of its caffeine). Because some of the flavor molecules end up in the water, too, the caffeine is removed from the water, and the water solution is added back to the beans to restore their flavor. Another decaffeination method is to soak the beans in hot water that already was used to soak a batch of coffee beans. Flavor molecules that leech out of the new batch are replaced by molecules already in the water. But the caffeine needs to be removed from the solution. One way to do that is by mixing methylene chloride or ethyl acetate with the beans' soaking water. Those chemicals combine with the caffeine and are then filtered or evaporated out of the water, taking the caffeine with them. These chemicals and procedures are also frequently used in tea decaffeination. Another way to remove caffeine from beans or tea leaves is by exposing them directly to liquid carbon dioxide, in which caffeine dissolves. Whatever the decaffeination method, flavor is best preserved when the beans or leaves are treated with a liquid containing as many of the natural plant substances as possible.

Dr. Roland Griffiths, a caffeine researcher at the Johns Hopkins School of Medicine, analyzed a huge array of studies about caffeine withdrawal and found that just 100 mg of caffeine a day—one average cup of coffee or two 12-ounce sodas—could create enough of a physical dependence so that people suffered from headaches, fatigue, and irritability without it. Some people, especially if they had been consuming a lot and stopped suddenly, reported flu-like symptoms including muscle pain, nausea, and vomiting. About 13 percent of people had a bad enough withdrawal period that they called in sick from work or couldn't do the day's tasks at home.

Among those studies were several that showed withdrawal problems in children. Kids who were accustomed to consuming caffeinated beverages had problems paying attention in school and remembering things when they stopped drinking caffeine. Withdrawal signs usually started the day after they stopped the beverages, and lasted up to a week afterward. That suggests schoolwork might suffer if kids who are accustomed to drinking caffeinated beverages don't get their daily dose. That degree of dependence among young people is something about which parents and health professionals are quite alarmed.

How Much Is Too Much?
Dr. Griffiths believes that even 10 mg of caffeine affects a person to a small degree. That's just a few

gulps of soda or a few sips of coffee. Of course, very few people are going to stop at that amount. After all, people want caffeine's stimulant effects. So how much is too much?

People's reactions to caffeine vary, as do their abilities to clear it from their systems after they have consumed it. The U.S. government doesn't have any official guidelines about how much caffeine is a "harmless" daily dose, but 300 mg is often stated as a recommended maximum for adults. That is the amount in about three cups of coffee or six 12-ounce servings of soda or tea.

Canada has come up with some guidelines for children, though, because nobody really knows what caffeine might be doing to kids' physical and mental development. The suggestion is that kids age seven to nine set a limit at about 60 mg of caffeine a day. That's equal to about 16 ounces of caffeinated soda. The recommendation for kids between ten and twelve years old is to consume no more than 85 mg daily. There are no special guidelines for older children.

It can be difficult to limit caffeine consumption to a certain level even if a person wishes to because there is no requirement that the actual amount be printed on beverages and foods. In addition, caffeine may be included in a form that most people won't recognize. It is up to a consumer to do some research if limiting caffeine—or going off it altogether—is a goal.

Easing Off Caffeine

For kids, a soft drink habit may be about the caffeine, but just as "addictive" is the social habit of drinking sodas. Wherever young people gather for some activity, there will almost certainly be soft drinks. And for many adults, it would be unthinkable to go without a morning caffeine kick before work, or during a break, or as an aid to keep working late into the night. Someone who decides to reduce or eliminate caffeine is facing a triple challenge: going without the stimulant effects of the caffeine, going without other ingredients in beverages or food that are pleasurable (like the sugar and flavorings), and going without the behavior associated with consuming caffeine. That last part may be the hardest to overcome.

Fortunately, there are some ways to cut caffeine. An obvious one is to choose decaffeinated replacements. All the most common beverages now come in decaffeinated forms. That makes it possible to continue with the habit of consuming a drink with a similar flavor, but without the drug component. And indeed, decaffeinated beverage consumption is on the rise. People may not be going completely without caffeine, but some are cutting back.

There are also coffee substitutes—beverage mixes that provide some flavor and look something like brewed coffee, but are made instead of other plant ingredients, such as roasted chicory root. People who adore coffee's flavor and aroma will say,

A DIET THAT IS RICH IN NUTRITION CAN HELP PROVIDE THE ENERGY ONE USED TO GET FROM CAFFEINE.

however, that these substitutes leave a lot to be desired. They may be tasty and hot, but are not decent replacements.

Another replacement for a hot caffeinated beverage is herbal tea. A wide variety of teas on the grocery store shelves these days are made of flowers,

leaves, roots, fruits, berries, spices, or other ingredients that don't contain caffeine. It is important to
realize that some are made with black or green tea
in addition to those other noncaffeinated ingredients. "Lemon tea," for example, comes in both an
herbal form with no caffeine, and a form that is regular (caffeinated) tea with some lemon flavor added.

Finding Energy without Caffeine
There are very effective ways to gain a sense of
energy besides consuming caffeine. Here are some
ideas:

- Exercise for ten minutes. Go for a walk,
  dance, do some aerobics, shoot some
  hoops, kick around a soccer ball. That
  activity tells the body to tap into its own
  energy supplies.
- If energy is waning while doing sedentary
  activity, such as homework or working at
  the computer, do something completely
  different for a few minutes, such as talking
  with a friend, working on a hobby, or going
  outdoors to get some fresh air.
- Substitute another food item or beveage—
  preferably something nutritious—when the
  urge for a caffeinated drink arises. Avoid
  snacks with a lot of sugar, because they can
  give a sense of energy for a while, then cause
  an energy "crash" an hour or two later.

• Take a brief nap. This doesn't work for everyone. Some people find a ten-minute nap revives their energy, though others find it makes them groggy for a long while afterward.

Daily energy lows are a sign that something isn't right that could be corrected. Some problems that may need fixing:

• Difficulty sleeping. Many different things can interfere with sleep (including too much caffeine during the day). Other problems may also make it harder to sleep well, such as too much noise in the house or outside, an uncomfortable bed or bedding, a room that is kept too hot, allergies, watching disturbing television programs or movies before bed, and eating a lot of food right before bedtime.

• Lack of exercise. People who participate in some type of physical exercise several times a week have more energy during the day. They also sleep better at night.

• Poor diet. A diet that is rich in nutritious foods provides the body with needed energy. Going without a meal, or replacing one with a soda or coffee, isn't a good choice for keeping one's body fit and able to tap into its own energy supplies when needed. Instead, regular meals and nutritious snacks will reduce the times when a caffeine kick feels like the only option.

- Depression or temporary "blues." If a person isn't happy with what's going on in his or her life, it is much harder to feel energized. Because caffeine improves a person's mood, it can help keep someone from falling into a dreary, hopeless state. But it shouldn't replace efforts to look at what's behind feelings of depression, boredom, or lack of interest in life. A counselor, good friend, respected adult, or parent can help.
- Physical illness or disease. Check with a doctor if low energy is often a problem and it isn't clear why. It may be caused by an illness or hormone imbalance that is easily improved with proper care.

One more idea about cutting back on caffeine: do it with friends. Making a pact with someone to achieve a certain goal can really work, and be much more enjoyable. And cut back gradually. Someone who has four sodas a day will probably find it easier to reduce that to three for a couple of weeks, then two, and so on, rather than to stop all consumption immediately. That gradual reduction will also minimize withdrawal symptoms.

The consumption of caffeinated beverages has met with disapproval sometimes in the past. Some disapproval continues today, mostly in the form of worry that habitual caffeine consumption is bad, especially for kids. In addition, some people want to keep their bodies free of anything that can create dependence. Caffeine remains, however, among the least dangerous and most widely enjoyed of available drugs, and will undoubtedly continue to be woven into the fabric of civilization for centuries to come.

GLOSSARY

addiction—The condition of having a physical need for a substance. See also *dependence*.

adenosine—A naturally occurring chemical in the body that causes a resting state, and that caffeine blocks.

alertness aids—Pills or other products, usually containing caffeine, that help keep a person awake and alert for several hours.

antioxidants—Substances in many plants that are thought to protect against disease, including cancer.

asthma—A lung disease in which the tubes that move air in and out of the lungs become narrowed, making breathing difficult.

cacao—The raw substance derived from the seeds of the cacao tree, also sometimes called cocoa (though that has other meanings as well).

chai—A traditional tea beverage from India made from black tea combined with milk, sweeteners, and spices.

dependence—The physical or psychological need for a substance that causes a person to devote much time, attention, and/or money to obtaining that substance. Physical dependence on a drug is a change in body chemistry that makes continued use of that drug necessary to avoid withdrawal symptoms. Psychological dependence is a powerful desire for a drug without physical symptoms if it isn't taken.

energy drink—A type of beverage that also often contains purified caffeine or caffeine-containing ingredients.

guarana—A plant that grows in the Amazon region of Brazil, the seeds of which are made into a popular hot beverage and soft drink in South America. The seeds contain more caffeine than coffee and have other methylxanthines as well.

herbal tea—A beverage made from various combinations of plant leaves, flowers, barks, roots, or fruits that do not contain caffeine.

jitters—A reaction to caffeine that includes restlessness, anxiety, shakiness, or difficulty concentrating.

maté—A plant indigenous to South America from which a caffeinated drink is made using the leaves.

mateine—A name given to the stimulant substance in maté, though it is caffeine.

metabolite—A chemical produced by the body as part of the breakdown process of another chemical.

methylxanthine—A type of molecule that consists of a xanthine structure to which methyl groups are attached. Caffeine, theobromine, and theophylline are methylxanthines.

paraxanthine—The most abundant metabolite of caffeine produced by the liver and which has stimulant properties (theobromine and theophylline are less abundant metabolites).

purine—A molecule with a double-ring structure that forms the basis for methylxanthines as well as some key molecules in living organisms such as DNA, RNA, and ATP (adenosine triphosphate, an energy molecule used by all cells).

soda fountain—An area in 1880s drugstores where the pharmacist would serve medicinal beverages, which in the 1900s came to include soft drinks.

stimulant—A substance that enhances alertness, energy, and a sense of well being.

tea—Any beverage made of plant leaves, flowers, roots, or other parts steeped in hot water. Tea often more specifically means a beverage made from the caffeine-containing plant *Camellia sinensis*, and comes in different forms which differ in how long the leaves are left to dry.

theobromine—A relatively weak stimulant related to caffeine and a metabolite of it, found in cacao.

theophylline—A stimulant related to caffeine found in tea in small amounts; a metabolite of caffeine.

tolerance—The condition in which a person's body becomes accustomed to a drug, so that, over time, the drug's effects become weaker. Higher doses are then needed to have the same effect that a lower dose once had.

withdrawal—The process of discontinuing the use of a drug, which can cause physical, emotional, or mental changes.

yoco—Another name for guarana.

FURTHER INFORMATION

Books

Kummer, Corby. *The Joy of Coffee: The Essential Guide to Buying, Brewing, and Enjoying*. Boston: Houghton Mifflin, 2003.

Lam, Kam Chuen, et al. *The Way of Tea: The Sublime Art of Oriental Tea Drinking*. Hauppauge, NY: Barron's Educational Series, 2002.

Rasmussen, Wendy, and Ric Rhinehart. *Tea Basics: A Quick and Easy Guide*. Hoboken, NJ: Wiley, 1998.

Web Sites

The Coffee Institute: Information on coffee around the world, including its relationship to the environment, politics, and societies.
http://www.coffeeresearch.org

History of Soft Drinks: Extensive background on the invention of nonalcoholic beverages.
http://inventors.about.com/library/weekly/aa091699.htm

Soft Drinks: America's Other Drinking Problem. A summary of concerns about soft drinks.
http://www.westonaprice.org/modernfood/soft.html

Tea Trail: Fun facts related to tea, especially for young people, from the United Kingdom.
http://www.teatrail.co.uk

BIBLIOGRAPHY

American Cancer Society. "Pancreatic Cancer Is Not Linked With Drinking Coffee or Alcohol." http://www.cancer.org/docroot/NWS/content/NWS_1_1x_Pancreatic_Cancer_Is_Not_Linked_With_Drinking_Coffee_or_Alcohol.asp

Angehagen, M., D. G. Margineanu, E. Ben-Menachem, L. Ronnback, E. Hansson, and H. Klitgaard. "Levetiracetam Reduces Caffeine-induced Ca2+ Transients and Epileptiform Potentials in Hippocampal Neurons." *Neuroreport* 14, no. 3 (2003): 471–475. http://www.ncbi.nlm.nih.gov/entrez/query.fcgi?cmd=Retrieve&db=pubmed&dopt=Abstract&list_uids=12634506&query_hl=13

Bellis, Mary. "Introduction to Pop: The History of Soft Drinks." About.com. http://inventors. about.com/od/foodrelatedinventions/a/ soft_drinks.htm

Bernstein, G. A., M. E. Carroll, N. W. Dean, R. D. Crosby, A. R. Perwien, and N. L. Benowitz. "Caffeine Withdrawal in Normal School-age Children." *Journal of the American Academy of Child and Adolescent Psychiatry* 37, no. 8 (1998): 858–865. http://www.ncbi.nlm.nih.gov/entrez/query.fcgi? cmd=Retrieve&db=PubMed&list_uids=9695448 &dopt=Abstract

Best, Ben. "Is Caffeine a Health Hazard?" http://www.benbest.com/health/caffeine.html

Canizaro, Mark C. "Xocoatl." http://www.xocoatl .org/history.htm

The Coffee Science Information Centre. "Coffee and Cancer." http://www.cosic.org/coffee-and-health/ cancer

Cromie, William J. "Coffee Won't Grind You Down: May Reduce Risk of Suicide, Study Concludes." *Harvard University Gazette.* http://www.news. harvard.edu/gazette/1996/03.14/CoffeeWont Grind.html

Erowid. "Does Yerba Maté Contain Caffeine or Mateine?" (Dec. 2003). http://www.erowid.org/ plantsyerba_mate/yerba_mate_chemistry1.shtml

The Field Museum. "The History of Chocolate." http://www.fieldmuseum.org/chocolate/history. html

Food and Agriculture Organization of the United Nations. "Annex Commodity Tables and Graphs." In *Commodity Market Review 2001-02.* http:// www.fao.org/documents/show_cdr.asp?url_file=/ DOCREP/005/Y3007E/y3007e07.htm

Gold, Alison K. "Caffeine and Bone: Does Coffee Consumption Contribute to Osteoporosis in Post-Menopausal Women?" http://www.focusanthro. org/Archive2001-02/caffeine_and_bone.htm #body1

Goodbody, John. "Tea and Coffee Back on the Menu for World's Athletes." *Times Online* Sept. 25, 2003). http://www.timesonline.co.uk/printFriendly /0,,1-4-830097,00.html

Health Canada. "Fact Sheet Caffeine and Your Health." http://www.hc-sc.gc.ca/fn-an/securit/ factsfaits/ caffeine_e.html

Inoue, Manami, Itsuro Yoshimi, Tomotaka Sobue, and Shoichiro Tsugane, for the JPHC Study Group. "Influence of Coffee Drinking on Subsequent Risk of Hepatocellular Carcinoma: A Prospective Study in Japan."

Joint Food Safety and Standards Group. "Survey of Caffeine and Other Methylxanthines in Energy Drinks and Other Caffeine-Containing Products (Updated)." Food Surveillance Information Sheet

Number 144 (March 1998), http://archive. food.gov.uk/maff/archive/food/infsheet/1998/ no144/144caff.htm

International Programme on Chemical Safety (IPCS) "Maté: Summary of Data Reported and Evaluation." *International Agency for Research on Cancer* 51 (1991); p. 273. http://www.inchem.org/ documents/iarc/vol51/03-mate.html

Jarvis, Gail. "The Rise and Fall of Cocaine Cola." LewRockwell.com. http://www.lewrockwell.com/ jarvis/jarvis17.html

Jenkins, Mark A. "Caffeine and the Athlete." SportsMed Web. http://www.rice.edu/~jenky/ sports/ caffeine.html

Juliano, Laura M., and Roland R. Griffiths. "Is Caffeine a Drug of Dependence?" *Psychiatric Times* 18, no. 2 (2001). http://www.psychiatrictimes.com/ p010247.html

Kummer, Corby. *The Joy of Coffee: The Essential Guide to Buying, Brewing, and Enjoying.* Boston: Houghton Mifflin, 2003.

Lleras, E. "Species of *Paullinia* with Economic Potential." In *Neglected Crops, 1492 from a Different Perspective,* ed. by Hernández Bermejo, J. E., and J. León, 223–228. Food and Agriculture Organization of the United Nations (1994). http://www.fao.org /docrep/t0646e/T0646E0m.htm#Species%20of %20*paullinia*%20with%20economic%20potential

Mathur, Ruchi. "Diabetes Mellitus." MedicineNet, Inc. http://www.medicinenet.com/diabetes_mellitus/article.htm

Murray, Michael, and Joseph Pizzorno. *Encyclopedia of Natural Medicine*. New York: Three Rivers Press, 1997.

Pendergrast, Mark. *Uncommon Grounds: The History of Coffee and How It Transformed Our World*. New York: Basic Books, 1999.

Raintree Nutrition Tropical Plant Database. "Guaraná." http://www.raintree.com/guarana.htm

Steer P. A., and D. J. Henderson-Smart. "Theophylline and Caffeine in Preterm Infants with Apnea." The Cochrane Collaboration. http://www.cochrane.org/reviews/en/ab000273.html

Strain E. C., G. K. Mumford, K. Silverman, and R. R. Griffiths. "Caffeine Dependence Syndrome: Evidence from Case Histories and Experimental Evaluations." *Journal of the American Medical Association*, 272, No. 13 (1994):1043-1048. (Table reproduced at http://www.psychiatrictimes.com/p010247.html)

Tavani A., and C. La Vecchia. "Coffee and Cancer: A Review of Epidemiological Studies, 1990–1999." *European Journal of Cancer Prevention* 9, no. 4 (2000): 241-256. http://www.ncbi.nlm.nih.gov/entrez/query.fcgi?cmd=Retrieve&db=PubMed&list_uids=10958327&dopt=Abstract

Tilling, Simon. "Caffeine." http://www.chm. bris.ac.uk/ webprojects2001/tilling/introduction.htm

Tindall, Randy. "The Culture of Cola: Social and Economic Aspects of a West African Domesticate." Southern Illinois University Carbondale Ethnobotanical Leaflets (December 1997). http://www.siu.edu/~ebl/leaflets/cola.htm

United States Food and Drug Administration. "The Story Of The Laws Behind The Labels." http://www.cfsan.fda.gov/~lrd/history1.html

Weinberg, Bennett A., and Bonnie K. Beale. *The World of Caffeine: The Science and Culture of the World's Most Popular Drug.* New York: Routledge, 2001.

Wilstar.com. "Caffeine Content Of Popular Drinks." http://wilstar.com/caffeine.htm

Wyatt, J. K., C. Cajochen, A. Ritz-De Cecco, C. A. Czeisler, and D. J. Dijk. "Low-dose Repeated Caffeine Administration for Circadian-phase-dependent Performance Degradation During Extended Wakefulness." *Sleep* 27, no. 3 (2004): 374–381. http://www.ncbi.nlm.nih.gov/entrez/ query.fcgi?cmd=Retrieve&db=pubmed&dopt =Abstract&list_uids=15164887&query_hl=5

INDEX

ABOUT THE AUTHOR

Lorrie Klosterman, Ph.D., is a biologist and a freelance writer and educator. Her books for Marshall Cavendish Benchmark include *Leukemia,* *Meningitis,* and *The Facts About Depressants.*